M.A.Fayzullaeva

# MOST EFFICIENT GAMES AND GAME-LIKE ACTIVITIES USED IN TEACHING
## Monograph

© Taemeer Publications LLC
**Most Efficient Games and Game-Like Activities used in Teaching**
by: Madina Fayzullaeva
Edition: February '2024
Publisher:
*Taemeer Publications LLC* (Michigan, USA / Hyderabad, India)

© **Taemeer Publications**

| | | |
|---|---|---|
| Book | : | Most Efficient Games and Game-Like Activities used in Teaching |
| Author | : | **Madina Fayzullaeva** |
| Publisher | : | Taemeer Publications |
| Year | : | '2024 |
| Pages | : | 90 |
| Title Design | : | *Taemeer Web Design* |

compiled by M.A.Fayzullaeva

Fayzullaeva M.A.

Most efficient games and game-like activities used in teaching. Monograph.

This monograph is devoted to the role of games in the activation and acceleration of teaching, especially in English. The monograph aims to introduce modern language learning opportunities that serve to activate the educational process and activities, and to develop the skills of teaching using games. Moreover, you can find information about popular methods which are appropriate for young learners, adolescents, adults, as well as, most efficient games and game-like activities used in teaching.

Reviewer:

***Dustnazar Khimmataliev,***

Professor of the Department of Pedagogy and Management, Chirchik state pedagogical university

***Nargiza Burieva,***

Associate professor, PhD on philological sciences of Jizzakh state pedagogical university

# CONTENTS

**CHAPTER I. POPULAR METHODS USED IN TEACHING**     11

1.1 Method appropriate for young learners – TPR     11

1.2 Method appropriate for adolescents - Direct Method     16

1.3 Method appropriate for adults - grammar-translation     20

**CHAPTER II. TYPES OF LEARNERS IN DIFFERENT AGE GROUPS**     24

2.1 Young learners, Characteristics of young learners     24

2.2 Adolescents, Characteristics of adolescent learners     27

2.3 Adults, Characteristics of adult learners     31

**CHAPTER III. MOST EFFICIENT GAMES AND GAME-LIKE ACTIVITIES USED IN TEACHING**     33

**3.1 Most efficient games and game-like activities used in teaching children**     **33**

**3.2 Most efficient games and game-like activities used in teaching adolescents**     **51**

**3.3 Most efficient games and game-like activities used in teaching adults**     **62**

**CONCLUSIONS**     **78**

**BIBLIOGRAPHY**     **80**

**APPENDICES**     **83**

# INTRODUCTION

President Islam Karimov stated in his speech at the opening ceremony of international conference ("Fostering a well-educated and intellectually advanced generation – critical prerequisite for sustainable development and modernization of country") "I would draw your attention to a rather vital point. In the system of education we attach a great importance to teaching pupils not merely liberal arts and vocational skills, but also required learning of foreign languages, for this is critical for them to maintain pro-active communication with their counterparts abroad, get extensive knowledge of everything that is going on around the globe, and command the august world of intellectual treasure". This work entitled "Game-like activities in Teaching" deal with the some extra any kind of activities. They are interesting and enjoyable for each age of learners. It is given extract from English and other countries analysis of the work on topic "Game-like activities in Teaching".

The aim of the work is to improve your knowledge in an easily way. Of course, it is up to you: How you know our skills with the helping by different game-like activities? Many edges of this theory had been studied, but I think, one of the methods of learning, free activities seldom had not been studied. It is given enough as specific theme yet. In this work we have studied the following theme with examples from the extract.

The work includes the following tasks:

1. To study the different approaches to the Games- activities

2. To study and discover the theory widely phraseological problems

3. To study the methods of variaty game- activities

4. To have a notion about free conversation

5. To try use the free speaking in condition that the given extract feelings

The work is studying to analyze the using the free translation in amazing of the extract for pupils. The theoretical value of the work. This work helps to enrich a basis in order to develop game activities as useful theory. While learning effectively so that you determine the different free conversation in respect of theoretical side, that's important part of the paper to look through all theories referring to that theme. The practical value of work is determined by the fact that its materials and the results can be used in the course of various game activities practical special courses on cognitive way.

The structure of the work is the work consists of

Introduction, three Chapters, Conclusion and the List of used literature. Introduction includes actuality, aim, tasks, analyze, theoretical and practical values of the work.

In chapter I the student of this work presents the most appropriate teaching methods. They are perceived as useful and successful. Each subsection describes the best teaching method for learners from the under-mentioned age groups. There is also the information about the techniques which are used in particular methods.

Chapter II defines the characteristics of young learners, adolescents and adults. It shows their advantages, e.g. their cognitive skills and other assets, and disadvantages, e.g. things they are afraid of and problems they may encounter during learning. The short and brief description of these different age groups of learners is also depicted in this chapter.

Chapter III contains the examples of games and game-like activities chosen as the most appropriate and efficient ones in teaching to different age groups. There are also particular descriptions how to play or use them during the lessons. The author also tries to prove that use of games and game-like activities is necessary at any age.

Conclusion is general last opinion about work.

List of used literature includes all the sources we

have used in our work.

English has become one of the most popular and common languages in the world. Its massive increase has been noticeable in the recent years. More and more people, regardless of their age. They obviously have different competences, skills and needs therefore, the topic which the author concentrates on, is Use of games and game-like activities in teaching to different age groups. There are three age groups mentioned: young learners (children aged between 5 or 6 and 12), adolescents (teenagers between 13 and 19) and adults. The age of learners is the major factor in teaching, however, games and game-like activities do not interfere in acquiring the language by people of different ages.

# CHAPTER I. POPULAR METHODS USED IN TEACHING

## 1.1 Method appropriate for young learners – TPR (Total Physical Response)

TPR is teaching method developed by Dr. James J Asher whose aim is to draw learners' attention and encourage them to respond to the given commands. TPR teaches vocabulary by using psychomotor systems. Thanks to the combination of tracing and rehearsal activities the probability of receiving a successful effect in teaching rises.

The method is believed to be perfect for teaching children and for using it as an additional technique during lessons. The method consists of coordination of two elements: speech and action. According to Asher, Total Physical Response is a natural way of teaching. He claims that the naturalistic processes should be reflected in teaching the second language and learning. Three central processes are based on this idea:

1) The listening competence is developed before speaking ability. It means that children, at the early phase of first language acquisition, are able to understand complex utterances before they gain the ability to produce them. Creation of the mental 'blueprint' of the language,

which was supposed to make spoken language production possible in the later phase of this listening, was taken into consideration by Asher.

Finlay, I. F. (1971). Translating. Edinburgh: The English University Press

1) Brislin, R. W. (1976). Translation: application and research. New York: Gardner Press

2) "children's ability in listening comprehension is acquired because children need to respond physically to spoken language in the form of parental commands; and"

3)"when a foundation in listening comprehension has been established, speech evolves naturally and effortlessly out of it"

According to Asher, to base the learning of foreign language upon the way in which children learn their native language is believed to be crucial techniques

Among the numerous techniques in Total Physical Response Method some of them are described:

4) Imperative drills are the major classroom activity in Total Physical Response. "They play an important role especially in eliciting the physical actions and activity on the part of the learners" (Richard at all. 1986). According to Asher, an instructor can teach vocabulary and most of grammatical structures of the target language using the

imperative (1997). The target language is used communicatively from the beginning of instruction; students listen to the teacher. Students do not speak at first, but the teacher's role is to help them to understand the point by showing pictures and occasionally using single words in children's native language; being as expressive as possible is also acceptable and welcome.

5) When all children are ready to respond to comments, and they do it correctly, the next step is introduced - one of those children is asked to give instruction to other classmates. It is crucial to remember that children speak when they are ready to do it; they are not and must not be forced to do so. The level of anxiety in the classroom is reduced and thanks to it student's self-confidence significantly rises. The creation of „low affective filter' is considered to be the learning condition when the classroom is full of good atmosphere; "The filter is kept low as well by the fact that students are not put on the spot to speak" (Larsen-Freeman, 2000). According to the following words, the absence of stress is really important in language acquisition "The learner is said to be liberated from self-conscious and stressful situations and is able to devote full energy to learning" (Richard at all. 1986).

6) Listening to tape-recorded words, phrases and sentences during looking at accompanying pictures is another technique in this method. It is the Winits and Reed's self-instructional program. The picture provides suitable context and because of it the meaning of the utterance is clear. Students are asked to respond to some questions by pointing at some pictures, but not using words. This exercise shows that they understand the language which they are listening; "Stories illustrated by pictures are also used as a device to convey abstract meaning" (Larsen-Freeman).

The Lexical Approach, developed by Lewis, is more concerned with receiving comprehensible input and is less concerned with students' production. It happens usually at lower levels when the teacher needs to talk extensively to the students and simultaneously do not get oral responses from them. The lexical exercises and activities are given to students to raise their awareness about lexical features about the target language. The phrasal lexicon of students can be developed by comprehensible input. Teachers talk abundantly to their students and simultaneously they do not require any responses from them. Thanks to the activities and exercises, which are given to the learners, students are encouraged to learn new phrases and notice lexical items. (Larsen-Freeman, 2000). Komorowska (2005) claims that This method is especially appropriate for completely early phases of teaching. However, there is a possibility to introduce, with the help of the skillful shaping of commands and progressive extend of them, really complicated grammar structures. For example: 'Anna, close the window! Mark when you see Anna has already closed the window - open the door' or 'If the window has already been closed-open the door, if not, leave it open'. - translated by Anna Peters.

## 1.2 METHOD APPROPRIATE FOR ADOLESCENTS - DIRECT METHOD

The Direct Method is one of the oldest methods of teaching. The main point of this method is not to use a native language. Teacher is not allowed to translate even a single word in students' mother tongue. The target language is the only one which should be used in the classroom. What is more, the meaning is directly conveyed through visual aids and the demonstrations. "Teachers must encourage direct and spontaneous use of the foreign language in the classroom" (Richard at all. 1986). The teacher can use the already known words, mime, demonstrations and pictures to present or explain new vocabulary rather than teach using the analytical procedures, mostly based on explanation of grammar structures and rules. Grammar is presented inductively. That means that students are obliged to figure out the rules on their own using the presented examples; teacher can never give to the students an explicit grammar. Using new vocabulary and grammar structures is practiced in complete sentences. Nonetheless, all four skills (writing, reading, listening, speaking) occur from the beginning, speaking skill is emphasized over the rest of them. As far as the oral communication is concerned, teaching vocabulary is really important (Larsen-Freeman, 2000).

According to Komorowska, this method is considered to be suitable for adolescents because they usually value dynamic interactive activities, which are typical of communicative approach, however, they also accept entertaining elements of TPR and the naturalness of the Direct Method. (Komorowska, 2005)

*Techniques*

There is a wide range of techniques used in the Direct Method. The following examples of techniques can definitely be useful for teachers and provide them more details.

*Question answer exercise*

To practice new vocabulary and grammar structures students are given a series of questions and they need to answer them using only the target language. There is also an opportunity to change roles and students can ask questions instead of answer them.

*Reading aloud*

Students are asked to read the particular sections of a passage or dialogue. They take turns. To make the meaning of the section clear teacher uses pictures, gestures and examples to help students understand the point.

### Conversation practice

Series of questions is given to students. To answer these questions correctly students need to understand them. The teacher asks questions to and about individual students. The teacher's questions have to include a particular grammar structure. Then students ask each other their own questions. It is important to use the same grammar structure as in the teacher's presentation.

### Dictation

A particular passage is read three times by the teacher. Firstly, the teacher reads the text at a normal speed of speaking (students just listen). Then the pace is slow enough to give students the chance to write down all the words they have heard (teacher makes appropriate pauses). The last time is read again at a normal speed in order to check the written words.

### Fill-in-the-blank exercise

The appropriate grammar structure is necessarily needed to write it in the correct blank. Students have to elicit the grammar rule from the examples or remember the practice from the previous lessons. All the items have to be in the target language and there is no presentation of grammar rules. Students insert correct form of the grammar structure into the blanks.

## *Getting students to self-correct*

The teacher has to support students if they make mistakes and also give them choice between what they said and this what he supplied for them. To correct students' mistakes in a different way teacher can repeat what they said and emphasize the mistake using the appropriate intonation. Changed teacher's voice should give students the signal that something is wrong. Another possibility for the teacher to elicit the mistake is to repeat student's sentence and make a pause just before the mistake. It gives information that the next word was mistaken.

## *Paragraph writing*

Chosen topic of the paragraph is given to the students. They need to write a paragraph using appropriate grammar structures, their own words and skills. They can use the reading passage of the particular lesson as a model or write it from memory (Larsen- Freeman, 2000).

## 1.3 METHOD APPROPRIATE FOR ADULTS – GRAMMAR TRANSLATION

Grammar-translation method is believed to be appropriate for teaching adults. "Demanding a sense of humor and mobility TPR is a method which doesn't have to suit all of the adults; many of them, especially the older ones, will insist on using grammar-translation methods or at least cognitive methods" (Komorowska, 2005). - translated by Anna Peters.

This not new method of teaching was firstly called the Classical Method. This name has special origin; grammar-translation method was used in the teaching of the classical languages like Greek or Latin. This method has been used by teachers for many years (Larsen-Freeman, 2000). Its aim is to teach vocabulary the grammar structures of the target language which will be helpful and useful in reading and understanding texts.

The best way to achieve this is reading and translating texts from the target language into mother tongue and the other way round. Detailed analyzing, explaining and commenting particular grammar structures and rules occur during these exercises. Texts, which are used to practice, are often written by the authors of course books or they are adapted literary texts

(Komorowska,2005).The following features of grammar-translation method also deserve to be described. Firstly, the target language is considered only on the base of the level of the sentence. Secondly, not much, or even no attention, is paid to the spoken language. Thirdly, the necessary thing in this method is the high level of accuracy (Harmer,2007)

*Techniques*

The following techniques are only the part of the whole range of these associated with the grammar-translation method. However, these ones are described by Larsen-Freeman as useful in this method.

*Translation of the literary passage*

Students are given a reading passage and they are asked to translate it from the target language into their native language. The reading passage can be an extract taken from the target language literature or it can even be a text carefully written by the teacher; if it is written by the teacher the appropriate grammar structures and vocabulary have to be included in it. Students' translation doesn't have to be only written, they can translate the passage orally. Idioms should be translated in a way that shows that students understand their meaning; not literally.

### *Reading comprehension questions*

After reading and understanding of the reading passage students are asked to answer questions, written in the target language, based on the given text. There are three groups of questions: in the first group of questions students are asked to answer them using the information contained in the particular text. In the second group students have to answer questions which are not directly placed in the text. Finally, the third group of questions force students to combine their own experience with the reading text.

### *Synonyms / antonyms*

The set of words is given to the students and they are asked to find antonyms or synonyms, depending on what the set of words contains, in the given text. Students can be also asked to define the set of words using their understanding of the text, it means to use context to get to know the meaning of the words.

### *Deductive application of rule*

Examples of the particular grammar structures and the grammar rules are presented together. Exception are given to each grammar rule. When the rule is understood by students, they are asked to use it in other examples.

### *Fill-in-the-blanks*

Some words in sentences are missed. They can appear in brackets. Students have to insert correct grammar structure or write some parts of speech like prepositions, adverbs or adjectives. All the items in brackets do not have to be in the target language, memorization

Students obligation is to remember all the possible lists they get from their teacher. Lists can contain vocabulary, which is given in the target language and its equivalents in the native language of the students, or grammatical paradigms (i.e. verb conjugations).

*Use words in sentences*

Students create completely new sentences using new vocabulary or grammar structures. They do this in order to present they understand the meaning and use of those.

*Composition*

Writing about a topic using the target language. Students are given particular topic by the teacher. Topic should be suitable to the lesson. Students can sometimes be asked to write the precis of the reading passage from the lesson instead of writing a composition (Larsen-Freeman)

# CHAPTER II. TYPES OF LEARNERS IN DIFFERENT AGE GROUPS

## 2.1 Young learners. Characteristics of young learners.

It is commonly believed that children learn a new language fast and efficiently. These who begin acquiring a foreign language early do not have so many problems with pronunciation. What is more, they have the possibility to imitate the teacher's accent very precisely. On the other hand, they become bored quickly and lose their concentration easily. No child is exactly the same; some children develop their language competence slower, some gradually, however, the following characteristics describe the average young learner between five and ten years old (Wendy A. Scott at all. 1995).

*Characteristics of young learners*

Enthusiasm for learning is intensively displayed by young learners. They are curious about everything what surrounds them and this positive attitude towards acquiring a foreign language should be praised. Apart from being interested in learning, young learners are able to understand and do many more things:

➢ they more often understand what is happening than the language used to describe the particular situation;

➢ their understanding is based not only on words but on what they see, hear or feel;

➢ they learn indirectly rather than directly;

➢ they can argue and even explain why they think what they think;

➢ they try to speak in a foreign language even if they do not understand individual words;

➢ they can use their imagination and also decide how they are going to do some activities;

➢ they are able to use a big number of intonations in their first language; (Harmer, 2007)

Nevertheless, children are not in the position to fulfill all expectations towards them. Their world differentiates from the real life. They are sometimes unable to distinguish fiction from fact. The following features show certain difficulties which young learners have:

o they hardly ever admit that they misunderstand something, and they cheerfully and confidently ensure adults they understand;

o they sometimes do not understand what the adults' conversation is about; adults sometimes have problems with understanding children too. The difference is that children do not ask any additional questions in order to find out the point; they make believe they understand it;

- the curriculum cannot be chosen by young language learners;
- concentration on an activity can be distracted rapidly as children can get easily become bored and lose their interest. That is why constant change of activities should appear during the lesson.

## 2.2 ADOLESCENTS. CHARACTERISTICS OF ADOLESCENTS

Adolescent learners are often perceived as problem students. The main reason confirming it is adolescence. The period in which teenagers look for their identities and their self-esteem hesitates. On the other hand, teenagers during this difficult time are characterized by passionate commitment. When they begin doing something they engage so much and dedicate themselves to it. According to Harmer (2007), thanks to these factors, including abstract thought, they can be perceived as the most exciting students of all (Harmer, 2007).

*Characteristics of adolescent learners*

Against the deceptive perception of today's teenagers, not all of them behave inappropriately. Most of them can understand that learning is needed in life, and additionally, accomplish the given tasks. What is more, they are able to discuss abstract issues with the teacher. According to Harmer (2007), "there is almost nothing more exciting than a class of involved young people at this age pursuing a learning goal with enthusiasm." The teacher's role is to encourage students to learn by preparing adequate materials concerning their interests or even "to provoke student engagement with material which is relevant and involving" (Harmer 2007: 84). The point is to encourage teenagers to respond to the text, or any other kind of material, with their own opinions, experiences or reflections. People at this age are sensitive and they can be easily humiliated. Thus, there is a risk to give them tasks which they are not able to do. The lack of the knowledge how to achieve a particular goal in the given task can contribute to the feeling of humiliation. Simultaneously, the teacher cannot forget about strengthening the students' self-esteem and being aware of their need for identity.

Another characteristic is that many teenagers want to be approved of their peers. They like feeling valued and they really take the negative opinions personally, especially these said by their contemporaries. Therefore, looking for respect among peers becomes most noticeable in teenagers. Harmer (2007) claims that this situation pertains to students, "who may not be very impressed by learning success but are often amused or amazed by the humor or anarchic behavior of their peers."

Motivation among teenagers is rather low. Teenage learners can be demotivated because they do not see the rewards or treat the learning of a foreign language as a trivial human need, which is a useless social skill. Komorowska (2005) claims that teenagers sometimes tend to resist. For example, they are rebellious when they think the texts, and other materials at school, are inadequate or simply useless. According to Brown (2007), motivation is divided into intrinsic and extrinsic. Intrinsically motivated learners have their own needs. They do their best to achieve what they have planned; they are goal-oriented. Those, with no inner expectations, who undertake the particular tasks only to receive an external reward are perceived as extrinsically motivated learners. Teachers can provide some authentic materials such as magazines, articles from the real newspapers, catalogues, website printouts and off-air video recordings to help teenagers become more motivated, Osborne (2005) claims teacher. According to Harmer (2007), "there is almost nothing more exciting than a class of involved young people at this age pursuing a learning goal with enthusiasm." The teacher's role is to encourage students to learn by preparing adequate materials concerning their interests or even "to provoke student engagement with material which is relevant and involving" (Harmer 2007). The point is to encourage teenagers to respond to the text, or any other kind of material, with their own opinions, experiences or reflections. People at this age are sensitive and they can be easily humiliated. Thus, there is a risk to give them tasks which they are not able to do. The lack of the knowledge how to achieve a particular goal in the given task can contribute to the feeling of humiliation. Simultaneously, the teacher cannot forget about strengthening the students' self-esteem and being aware of their need for identity.

But not only the good rapport with friends are desired. The teacher's approval makes teenagers happy and satisfied. When the teacher stops showing his approval, the students' behavior can change for worse. As pointed out by Osborne (2005), treating teenagers as equals and careful listening to them is considered to be a good way in teaching adolescents.

For example, they are rebellious when they think the texts, and other materials at school, are inadequate or simply useless. According to Brown (2007), motivation is divided into intrinsic and extrinsic. Intrinsically motivated learners have their own needs. They do their best to achieve what they have planned; they are goal-oriented. Those, with no inner expectations, who undertake the particular tasks only to receive an external reward are perceived as extrinsically motivated learners. Teachers can provide some authentic materials such as magazines, articles from the real newspapers, catalogues, website printouts and off-air video recordings to help teenagers become more motivated, Osborne (2005) claims.

## 2.3 ADULTS. CHARACTERISTICS OF ADULT LEARNERS.

Adulthood - the period of being mature, more serious and balanced. This is the moment in life in which adult language learners have a range of life experience, and what is more, they can share it with the other students in a group. Teaching grownups is perceived as not so demanding as teaching children, because most of adults tend to be more disciplined (Harmer, 2007).

*Characteristics of adult learners*

There are many special characteristics concerning adult language learners. Some of them are really helpful during classes, but some part of them is rather offending or even worrying. The following characteristics are the positive ones:

- a wide range of life experience, bringing by the adult learners into the classroom, allow teachers to use various activities during the classes; the topics can be miscellaneous;
- they are much more disciplined than children or adolescents. Their teachers do not have to deal with the daily discipline problems. Adults also cooperate willingly and they are expected to do it immediately;
- adults learners' expectations are taken seriously.

They mostly come to the classes with a long history of language learning experience. Thanks to these experiences, whatever they are good or bad, grownups have got the possibility to form opinions about how both, learning and teaching, should be accomplished;

Most of them is motivated intrinsically, knows the reason of learning and treat it with the great importance. Their attention span is rather long and they are able to continue the lesson despite being bored. (Harmer, 2007).

# CHAPTER III. MOST EFFICIENT GAMES AND GAME-LIKE ACTIVITIES USED IN TEACHING TO DIFFERENT AGE GROUPS

## 3.1 Most efficient games and game-like activities used in teaching children.

As the author of this work mentioned in the second chapter each group of learners has a variety of characteristics and skills which can be divided in terms of age. With the help of theirs' description the author presents the most efficient games and game-like activities used in teaching in different age groups.

*Songs*

Thanks to singing songs children have the possibility to get to know or practice the rhythm, tone and melody. Songs improve children's listening skills, teach vocabulary and encourage children to express themselves during singing (Mac Naughton at all. 2004). Undermentioned examples present the ways in which the song can be used. The aim of these activities is to practice vocabulary, language point and listening skills.

*Find the word*

The task for young learners here is to listen for a certain word or words and then count their number in a particular song. For example, children can count words "hello" and "goodbye" in the song "Hello, goodbye" by the Beatles (Phillips, 1993. See appendix no. 1)

*Song pictures 1*

To prepare this exercise the teacher needs a descriptive text of the song and a picture which illustrates it. The picture can be found or drawn and it can have some mistakes or gaps. Then, children get the copies, listen to the song and they correct or complete the picture. (Phillips, 1993)

*Song picture 2*

A song that tells the story is needed. The teacher draw simple pictures to illustrates the story, cut them out and make a worksheet. The sequence of the pictures has to be out of order. The children's role is to listen to the song and put the pictures in the correct order. (Phillips, 1993)

*Gap fill song*

An important thing to do is to choose the song with the clear words in its text.

*Picture gaps*

The teacher substitutes the real words from the song for some of the pictures. Students' task is to write the full name of the thing from the picture to complete the song. For example:

Fig. 1. An example of a picture gap (Phillips, 1993).

*Adjective fill*

The teacher chooses the song with a big number of adjectives which can be changed easily. Children listen to the song and draw a picture of it. Next they change the adjectives and draw a picture of a new description. This exercise can be also used with the written texts and descriptions. (Phillips, 1993)

*Physical activities*

Thanks to the group work children can work at the same time, the language practice time increases and "children are less likely to become bored or lose interest because they are actively involved." (Toth, 1995). These examples present how to avoid boredom during the classes.

*The washing line game*

Before the game starts, the teacher should check the conversance of the children's vocabulary. The short length of rope has to be held between two learners in order to create a washing line.

Fig. 2. The washing-line game (Halliwell, 1992)

The rest of the class is divided into two teams and their representatives are chosen to come to the front. Pupils' task is to pick out the object which the teacher asked them to bring. Pupils have to listen to the teacher's commands and bring the desirable thing. They look for it in beforehand prepared boxes. The pupil who hangs an object on a line first is the winner and scores a point for his or her team.

Fig. 3. The washing-line game (Halliwell, 1992)

This activity provides the revision of particular words rather than the whole phrases (Halliwell, 1992).

*Body writing*

This exercise is used to associate students with spoken or written forms of letters, numbers, words or shapes. Children can work in groups or -individually. Their task is to make shapes of particular figures with their bodies. Apart from revision of alphabet and vocabulary, this exercise provide the ability of co-operation between the students. To form the letters with their bodies, students can stand up or lie down. If children are not divided into groups yet, the teacher can start from the warming-up exercises. He or she should start from the simple letters, like I or T, which child can build on his or her own. Next, the teacher can go on to more difficult letters, like A or M, which demand co-operation between the members of the team (Phillips, 1993).

*"Disco routine"*

Another energetic activity which can be used to revise the body parts and the phrases concerning this category of words. This activity is similar to the game "Simon says."

What the teacher has to do first is to refresh vocabulary using action words, e.g. 'stamp', 'point', 'shake', etc. Children obey and copy the teacher's commands. Then the game 'Simon says' can be used as a warm-up exercise. The teacher say 'Simon says' and he or she gives the instruction. The teacher can start the game with the 'stand up' command, if the children make a mistake they have to sit down. The next step is writing up the teacher's disco routine on the board and doing it with the children and chosen music.

> Fig. 4. The example of a "Disco routine" (Halliwell, 1992)

Then children are divided into pairs and try to make up and write down their own routine, consisting of four actions. The teacher goes around and helps them. The teacher collects pupils' papers, in order to check if there are any major mistakes, so they need to write their names at the top of them (Halliwell, 1992).

(Scott at all. 1995) 10 Best ESL Games for Teachers Abroad

Emma Lander
**TOPIC EXPERT**

Emma is a freelance copy and content writer. She is a qualified EFL teacher and has taught in the UK, Scandinavia and South Korea.

Photo credit: Marco, Himalayan Education Lifeline Programme Alum

Games and fun activities are a vital part of teaching. Whether you're teaching adults or children, games will liven up your lesson and ensure that your students will leave the classroom wanting more.

Games can be used to warm up the class before your lesson begins, during the lesson to give students a break when you're tackling a tough subject, or at the end of class when you have a few minutes left to kill. There are literally hundreds, probably thousands, of games that you can play with your students. EFL games are used to test vocabulary, practice conversing, learn tenses - the list is endless.

This list of ten classic ESL games every teacher

should know will help get you started and feeling prepared. Having these up your sleeve before stepping into the classroom will ensure your lessons run smoothly, and, should things get a little out of control, you'll be able to pull back the attention of the class in no time.

Want to jump right into the list? Here are the top 10 games we think your students will love:

- Board Race
- Call My Bluff / Two Truths and A Lie
- Simon Says
- Word Jumble Race
- Hangman
- Pictionary
- The Mime
- Hot Seat
- Where Shall I Go?
- What's My Problem?

Don't have a job yet? Check our teaching job board for the latest openings around the world!

1. Board Race

There isn't an EFL teacher I know who doesn't use this game in the classroom. Board Race is a fun game that is used for revising vocabulary, whether it be words from the lesson you've just taught or words from a lesson you taught last week. It can also be used at the start of the class to get students active. It is a great way of testing what your students already know about the subject you're about to teach.

Why use it? Revising vocabulary; grammar

Who it's best for: Appropriate for all levels and ages

How to play:

First, watch this helpful video of real teachers using this game in the classroom by Bridge TEFL:

This is best played with 6 students or more - the more, the better. I've used it in classes ranging from 7-25 years of age and it's worked well in all age groups. Here's a step by step explanation:

Split the class into two teams and give each team a colored marker.

If you have a very large class, it may be better to split the students into teams of 3 or 4.

Draw a line down the middle of the board and write a topic at the top.

The students must then write as many words as you require related to the topic in the form of a relay race.

Each team wins one point for each correct word. Any words that are unreadable or misspelled are not counted.

## 2. Call My Bluff / Two Truths and A Lie

Call My Bluff is a fun game which is perfect at the start of term as a 'getting to know you' kind of game. It is also a brilliant ice breaker between students if you teach classes who do not know one another -- and especially essential if you are teaching a small class size.

The game is excellent for practicing speaking skills, though make sure you save a time for after the game to comment on any mistakes students may have made during the game. (I generally like to reserve this for after the game, so you don't disrupt their fluency by correcting them as they speak).

With older groups you can have some real fun and you might be surprised what you'll learn about some of your students when playing this particular EFL game.

Why use it? Ice-breaker; Speaking skills

Who it's best for: Appropriate for all levels and ages but best with older groups

How to play:

Write 3 statements about yourself on the board, two of which should be lies and one which should be true.

Allow your students to ask you questions about each statement and then guess which one is the truth. You might want to practice your poker face before starting this game!

If they guess correctly then they win.

Extension: Give students time to write their own two truths and one lie.

Pair them up and have them play again, this time with their list, with their new partner. If you want to really extend the game and give students even more time to practice their speaking/listening skills, rotate partners every five minutes.

Bring the whole class back together and have students announce one new thing they learned about another student as a recap.

3. Simon Says

This is an excellent game for young learners.

Whether you're waking them up on a Monday morning or sending them home on a Friday afternoon, this one is bound to get them excited and wanting more. The only danger I have found with this game is that students never want to stop playing it.

Why use it? Listening comprehension; Vocabulary; Warming up/winding down class

Who it's best for: Young learners

How to Play:

Stand in front of the class (you are Simon for the

duration of this game).

Do an action and say Simon Says [action]. The students must copy what you do.

Repeat this process choosing different actions - you can be as silly as you like and the sillier you are the more the children will love you for it.

Then do an action but this time say only the action and omit 'Simon Says'. Whoever does the action this time is out and must sit down.

The winner is the last student standing.

To make it harder, speed up the actions. Reward children for good behavior by allowing them to play the part of Simon.

4. Word Jumble Race

Photo credit: Inne, African Impact volunteer in Zambia Alum

This is a great game to encourage team work and bring a sense of competition to the classroom. No matter how old we are, we all love a good competition and this game works wonders with all age groups. It is perfect for practicing tenses, word order, reading & writing skills and grammar.

Why use it? Grammar; Word Order; Spelling; Writing Skills

Who it's best for: Adaptable to all levels/ages

How to play:

This game requires some planning before the lesson.

Write out a number of sentences, using different colors for each sentence.

I suggest having 3-5 sentences for each team.

Cut up the sentences so you have a handful of words.

Put each sentence into hats, cups or any objects you can find, keeping each separate.

Split your class into teams of 2, 3, or 4. You can have as many teams as you want but remember to have enough sentences to go around.

Teams must now put their sentences in the correct order.

The winning team is the first team to have all

sentences correctly ordered.

5. Hangman

This classic game is a favorite for all students but it can get boring quite quickly. This game is best used for 5 minutes at the start to warm the class up or 5 minutes at the end if you've got some time left over. It works no matter how many students are in the class.

Why use it? Warming up / winding down class

Who it's best for: Young learners

How to play:

In case you've never played, here's a quick rundown.

Think of a word and write the number of letters on the board using dashes to show many letters there are.

Ask students to suggest a letter. If it appears in the word, write it in all of the correct spaces. If the letter does not appear in the word, write it off to the side and begin drawing the image of a hanging man.

Continue until the students guess the word correctly (they win) or you complete the diagram (you win).

6. Pictionary

This is another game that works well with any age group; children love it because they can get creative in the classroom, teenagers love it because it doesn't feel like they're learning, and adults love it because it's a break from the monotony of learning a new language - even though they'll be learning as they play.

Pictionary can help students practice their vocabulary and it tests to see if they're remembering the words you've been teaching.

Why use it? Vocabulary

Who it's best for: All ages; best with young learners

How to play:

Before the class starts, prepare a bunch of words and put them in a bag.

Split the class into teams of 2 and draw a line down the middle of the board.

Give one team member from each team a pen and ask them to choose a word from the bag.

Tell the students to draw the word as a picture on the board and encourage their team to guess the word.

The first team to shout the correct answer gets a point.

The student who has completed drawing should then nominate someone else to draw for their team.

Repeat this until all the words are gone - make sure you have enough words that each student gets to draw at least once!

7. The Mime

Miming is an excellent way for students to practice their tenses and their verbs. It's also great for teachers with minimal resources or planning time, or teachers who want to break up a longer lesson with something more interactive. It's adaptable to almost any language point that you might be focusing on.

This game works with any age group, although you

will find that adults tire of this far quicker than children. To keep them engaged, relate what they will be miming to your groups' personal interests as best as possible.

Why use it? Vocabulary; Speaking

Who it's best for: All ages; best with young learners

How to play:

Before the class, write out some actions - like washing the dishes - and put them in a bag.

Split the class into two teams.

Bring one student from each team to the front of the class and one of them choose an action from the bag.

Have both students mime the action to their team.

The first team to shout the correct answer wins a point.

Repeat this until all students have mimed at least one action.

8. Hot Seat

This is one of my students' favorite games and is always at the top of the list when I ask them what they want to play. I have never used this while teaching ESL to adults, but I imagine it would work well.

Hot Seat allows students to build their vocabulary and encourages competition in the classroom. They are also able to practice their speaking and listening skills and it can be used for any level of learner.

Why use it? Vocabulary; Speaking and Listening

Who it's best for: All ages and levels

How to play:

Split the class into 2 teams, or more if you have a large class.

Elect one person from each team to sit in the Hot Seat, facing the classroom with the board behind them.

Write a word on the board. One of the team members of the student in the hot seat must help the student guess the word by describing it. They have a limited amount of time and cannot say, spell or draw the word.

Continue until each team member has described a word to the student in the Hot Seat.

## 3.2 MOST EFFICIENT GAMES AND GAME-LIKE ACTIVITIES USED IN TEACHING ADOLESCENTS

Teenagers mature, begin to understand and learn more about the world. What is more, intellectual, motor or social skills are developed by children when they get older. A wider gamut of topics can be used to teach teenagers; one way or another, it is a good idea to use topics related to their world. (Osborne, 2002)

*Noughts and crosses*

To prepare materials needed to this game the teacher should draw a noughts and crosses grid on the board. Numbers from 1 to 9 should be written in each square and the class must be divided into two teams: X and O. The teacher thinks about the category of questions which he or she will ask during the game. The questions can concern anything e.g. general knowledge, questions or the previous unit in the students' course book. The next step belongs to students. They choose the square and answer the teacher's question. If they answer correctly, they get a symbol written in the chosen square. The line of three identical symbols, in any direction, have to appear on the grid. The first team to get this line is the winner.

If the teacher has no more ideas of questions he or

she can tell students to write new questions for the opposing team. That will be great practice in question formation.

*Making sentences*

This game provides the practice of the sentence production and formation. It also encourage students to use their creativity. To prepare this game correctly the teacher should cut out approximately 40 words from the magazines or newspapers and make sure of the balance of parts of speech. Then he or she sticks them on a sheet of paper in random order. See appendix no. 2

Then the teacher divides class in groups of up to four and gives them the copies of the set of words. Their task is to build the sentences consisting of: three words (e.g. Radio is free), four words (e.g. Most parents are happy) and five words (Cows enjoy politics in April). Students get seven minutes to create these sentences, the time depends on the complexity of task and level.

There is sometimes no need to motivate them, for example, by playing games or singing songs. But if these people are on a full-time course or study in the same kind of class for a long time they get bored sooner or later. Harmer claims "We won't want to treat them like children, but some of them might, nevertheless, respond well to a lighter style of learning which does, indeed, involve quizzes, puzzles and the study of contemporary songs" (Harmer, 1998).

*Puzzles*

Explaining what you mean

This vocabulary game, presented by Harmer, helps students with vocabulary they can use when they do not know the exact words to describe a particular thing. What students have to do is to read some descriptions and say or guess what is being described. Their answers can be checked with words situated at the bottom of the page. The next step can be a practice exercise in which students have to reorder words to make sentences and match them with the pictures. See appendix no. 3 Draw puzzle shapes on the back of each picture (4-5 shapes) and cut out the picture pieces.

Give each student in the class a jigsaw piece. They must not show their piece to anyone.

Students then mingle and question each other about what is on their puzzle piece to try and find people with pieces of the same jigsaw.

The object of the game is to find all pieces and put together the jigsaw. The first complete picture puzzle wins.

Something in common or 'give me five'

Explain that we can all find something in common with those around us. The object of this game is to discover as many things you have in common with fellow students. You can limit this to 5 things in common.

Brainstorm examples with the whole class, noting suggestions, e.g.

We both have long-haired cats

They both went to see Robbie Williams in concert

We all like Harry Potter

We both have a younger sister called Georgia

Our favourite colour is green

Our families go to the same supermarket, church, club, holiday place

*We both believe in love at first sight, ghosts, god.*

Give students a time limit to mingle and find out as many things they have in common. The one who finds the most is the winner.

Alternatively ask them to find five things and the first person to shout 'five' is the winner.

Create a biography

Take a biography of a famous person and write each detail on strips of paper.

Keep the identity secret so they have to guess, if

appropriate.

Draw a table on the board for students to copy and make notes e.g. place of birth, early years, famous for..

Give out the strips (split the class in two if large and give out 2 sets).

Students mingle and ask each other questions until they have as many details as possible about the person.

Take away the strips and put students in pairs or small groups to use their table of notes to write the biography.

These activity ideas originally appeared on the British Council Language Assistant website. Hide Tags

The reasons for using poetry are similar to those for using songs and many activities that you do with songs can be adapted to poetry.

Author: Jo Budden

Then students are divided into groups and asked to make a list of words from a particular category allotted to their team and draw them. Now students describe things for each other by taking part in an information-gap activity. Learners work in pairs. There are two crosswords needed in this activity, one for student A and for student B. Students' task is to describe, define or explain the words in the crossword. They are not allowed to use their exact names. For example, when student A asks student B what 1 down is, student B may reply: It is stuff you make candles with and it is sticky when it is hot. (Harmer, 2007: 232-233)

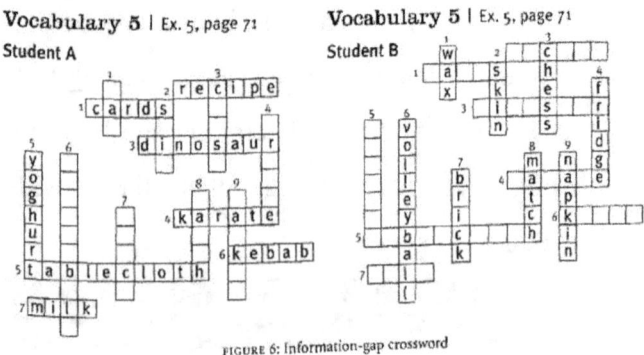

FIGURE 6: Information-gap crossword

Fig. 5. The example of a crossword (Harmer, 2007).

This activity is very similar to a describing game. Students can also be divided into groups or pairs. They are given three category of words or phrases. A set of cards face down or in an envelope is given to each group. The teacher demonstrates the activity by choosing a word from one of the vocabulary sets and describing it to the class until someone guesses the word. The most important thing is that students cannot use the word on the card in their card.

### Where Shall I Go?

This game is used to test prepositions of movement and should be played after this subject has been taught in the classroom. This game is so much fun but it can be a little bit dangerous since you'll be having one student in each pair be blindfolded while the other directs them. So make sure to keep your eyes open!

It is also excellent for the adult EFL classroom, or if you're teaching teenagers.

Why use it? Prepositions; Speaking and Listening

Who it's best for: All ages and levels

How to play:

Before the students arrive, turn your classroom into a maze by rearranging it. It's great if you can do this outside, but otherwise push tables and chairs together and move furniture to make your maze.

When your students arrive, put them in pairs outside the classroom. Blindfold one student from each pair.

Allow pairs to enter the classroom one at a time; the blindfolded student should be led through the maze by their partner. The students must use directions such as step over, go under, go up, and go down to lead their partner to the end of the maze.

What's My Problem?

Christmas is an excellent theme for adding games and fun to your teaching. Most students enjoy festive lessons if your activities encourage a personal contribution about the students' own families and customs.

Author: Clare Lavery

You can deal with the following aspects:

*History*

The religious background and/or specific background to the customs associated with the festival e.g. St Nicholas, the use of Carols or the introduction of the Christmas Tree or card giving in the UK.

Younger learners can make a Xmas card following your instructions, colour in a card following your instructions and write greetings in the card.

Lower levels can make the origins of or background to Xmas into an easy quiz which is much easier to read and do than a heavy text. Example question: Where does the custom of Xmas trees come from? What is another name for Father Christmas? How many days are there on an advent calendar?

Higher levels can pick a very simple carol. Jumble the couplets or miss out key words which students would understand. Don't dwell on every word or translate in detail but enjoy the sound and, with a willing group, sing. Use a history of Christmas text as a short group summary activity. Divide the text into 3. Each student in a group of 3 reads one part. Take away text and they make a summary of the origins of Christmas or they make questions together to challenge the rest of the class.

*Customs and traditions*

Look at customs surrounding gift giving (it differs in each country) and the types of celebration or worship associated e.g. parties in offices, pantomimes, carol concerts and carol singing around towns. Customs like using crackers during/after the meal are fascinating for students (especially if you can take a real cracker to show them).

Younger learners/lower levels can follow the

instructions to make a cracker in groups of 4.

Higher levels can look at the types of jokes and language in Christmas crackers.

### *Food and drink*

Describe the Christmas meal and traditional food eaten in the UK (e.g. mince pies). Pictures, photos or the real thing essential for this topic! Guess the weight of the pudding and its ingredients! Draw on your own family experience as much as possible.

Younger learners can draw their favourite/ideal Xmas meal and write words to label their picture.

Lower and higher levels can write a Xmas recipe in groups for a local Xmas dish or plan their perfect party in groups.

### *Songs and carols*

Students enjoy singing along to versions of carols they already sing in their own language (e.g. Silent Night) or songs which are well known from the chart CDs blasting out of every supermarket sound system ! Some songs lend themselves to a variety of activities e.g. The 12 Days of Christmas – match pictures to the correct numbers, illustrate the song, sing it around the class with one pair of students for each line or students make their own version with presents they would like to get over the

12 Days.

*Traditional poems and literature*

Younger learners can read the very funny nativity story 'Jesus's Christmas Party' by Nicholas Allen. It is brilliant for acting out and retelling through the pictures. The events are seen through the eyes of an angry innkeeper who is disturbed all night by the goings on in his stable. Raymond Brigg's 'The Snowman' is good for exploitation and the video has no dialogue so conversations can be invented by students or they can give a running commentary of what is happening in the story.

## 3.3 THE MOST EFFICIENT GAMES AND GAME-LIKE ACTIVITIES USED IN TEACHING ADULTS

Adults represent the group of learners which see the point of learning definitions. Learners play the game taking turns. The teacher tells students to do not interrupt anybody's description.1

*Quizzes*

Test your general knowledge. This is one of a lot of examples of quizzes which can be used to learn adults. The aim of this quiz is to revise articles, check what students have remembered and by the way test their general knowledge. Students work in pairs. Each pair gets one sheet. The teacher has to set a time limit to each exercise. In the first exercise, students complete the quiz with the articles; in the second one they try to answer as many questions as they can.

The next example of a quiz is a quiz concerning idioms. The students' task is easy. They have to read the questions and write their answer on a separate piece of paper. The main aim of this activity is to revise vocabulary - idioms. (Watcyn - Jones, 1993). See appendix no. 6.

To conclude, every age group needs a particular attention in teaching, special methods, techniques and furthermore games or game-like activities. There is no denying that the group of children is the most demanding one, but other groups cannot be forgotten. The proper selection of these can cause that the lesson is more interesting and students become more involved. Any authentic material exposes students and can be very motivating for your students, provided they are supported throughout the task. The other great thing about poems is for students to have the opportunity to see the language work creatively and freely. Poems can be used in many different ways and the more you use them the more uses you'll find for them.

*Where can I get the poems from?*

Finding poems to use is now incredibly easy with the internet. You can find lots of poems by simply typing in the author and the first line or title. There's a site called Poem Hunter which makes this even easier. So even if you only remember a few lines of a poem that you like you'll probably be able to find it. The site is http://www.poemhunter.com/

If you make worksheets using the poem be sure to acknowledge the author's name and the source.

How do I choose the right one for my class?

The first thing to consider when you're selecting a

poem for your class is the level of language. If you end up having to explain every single word then the poem may well lose its spark. On the other hand, students won't need to understand every word to get the general idea of most poems so don't be put off if you think the language level is slightly above what they would normally be able to handle. As with songs, if the students are supported throughout and are pre-taught some of the vocabulary, or given some visual aids to help them, they will be able to tackle more challenging texts than they are used to.

*What activities can I do with a poem?*

Introduce a topic

Poems can be a really nice way into a topic. A colleague recently recommended using a poem called The Ghoul by Jack Perlutsky as a way to introduce a Halloween lesson. He had made a gap fill by taking out the rhyming words. The students loved the poem and later on we took it in turns reading out the verses with the correct intonation and taking care to make the rhyming words rhyme. (Thanks to Johnny Lavery for this idea.)

To introduce the topic of old people and talking about grandparents in a class I've used Jenny Joseph's poem called Warning. The language is simple and the ideas are clear and can easily be supported with visual aids for very low levels.

These are just a few examples of linking a poem to a topic. By using a poem as a spring board into a topic you will make the class memorable for your students.

*Ordering the poem*

When you have chosen a suitable poem for your class, copy it onto a worksheet and cut up the verses. If the poem tells a story and the order is logical, ask student to read the verses and put them into the correct order. If the order isn't obvious, you can read out the poem and they can listen and put it into order as you read. From here you can go onto to look at the vocabulary, the rhyming words or to talking about the meaning of the poem.

*Rhyming words*

Obviously, some poems lend themselves well to looking at pronunciation. Whether you want to focus on individual sounds, rhyming pairs, connected speech or intonation patterns, poems can be a great way into it. Getting students to read out chunks of a poem as they copy the way you say it can be excellent practise for their pronunciation.

If you have higher levels and really want to get them thinking about pronunciation try the Pronunciation Poem which can be found on the Learn website. Practise saying it to yourself a few times before the class. It's harder than it looks!

### The Pronunciation Poem

Here is some pronunciation.

> Ration never rhymes with nation,
> Say prefer, but preferable,
> Comfortable and vegetable.
> B must not be heard in doubt,
> Debt and dumb both leave it out.
> In the words psychology,
> Psychic, and psychiatry,
> You must never sound the p.
> Psychiatrist you call the man
> Who cures the complex, if he can.
> In architect, chi is k.
> In arch it is the other way.

### Learn a verse

Once you have chosen the poem and have worked with it with your class, encourage the students to learn one verse by heart. It can be really motivating for younger students to be able to say perfectly. Ensure that they want to learn it and that it has some useful language in it which will be helpful in the future. Try not to get students to memorize chunks of language just for the sake of it or because you want to fill in the last few minutes and have run out of activities! However, it can be really satisfying for students to be able to be able to say a nice chunk of language and to be sure that their pronunciation is good, as they will have practiced it with you.

### *Record the students*

Getting students to record themselves saying a poem can be a nice way to help them improve their pronunciation. You could put students into pairs or small groups and get each student to read out aloud one of the verses of the poem. Then listen back to it in the class.

### *Write a new verse*

If you are teaching higher levels you could ask the students to create a new verse for the poem or to change one of the existing verses. This would be a challenging activity for most students so make sure you offer ideas and help to support students through the task. Be ready to give an example verse to show them that it's do-able!

### *Role play – dialogues*

If the poem you are using has any dialogue, you could use it as a springboard into a role-play. Poems with characters can also be used to inspire role-plays. An example of a poem that would be good for this is A Bad

Habit by Michael Rosen.

For most teacher poems are an under exploited resource that we have available to us. Although introducing your students to a poem or two throughout the course will take a lot of thought and a bit of preparation time on your side, I think it will be worth it.

*Discussion/speaking topics*

Does Santa exist?

Is it a good idea to encourage children to believe in Santa Claus ? Many sites on the net encourage this, with e-mail to the North Pole. How do students feel about this? Harmless fun or a cruel hoax to get kids to be good? When did they discover Santa didn't exist? Is he really necessary? Younger learners can say what they want for Xmas and then write a short email to Santa for fun.

My ideal present / My earliest Christmas memory / my best Christmas ever

(Where? When? Who with? Activities? Past or future?). Start with an example of your own and put headings on the board to show how you develop your ideas e.g. description of the place/ the weather and the year, your age/ the people spending Xmas with you/the best things you saw or did. Give students time to collect their own ideas. With lower levels run through the types of questions to ask, eliciting example replies around the class. Higher levels can have more freedom but encourage and practice the language needed for showing interest (Really?) and/or the language needed to encourage the speaker to expand on what they are saying (That's amazing/interesting. Do you always do that at Xmas?)

*My ideal Christmas Day*

(Who with? Where? What would you do?) Better with higher levels where you can encourage use of the second conditional . Do a brainstorm exercise first. Where are all the possible places to spend Xmas? (get suggestions- also wacky and unusual destinations so they get the idea) Ask them if they are sociable or quiet. Do you want a Xmas in a crowd or a Xmas with just one special person? Give examples of Xmas in another part of the world, such as Australia (see the link below) . Are you very keen on tradition or do you hate trees and all the Xmas over eating? A complete brainstorm will make this a more rewarding activity.

Then get students to interview at least 2 people about their ideal Xmas or give them a questionnaire: Find someone who would spend Xmas abroad/ alone/ not on this planet / in a strange place / with lots of people / in a very traditional way.

The whole class can then exchange their ideas and complete the questionnaire. This can be very funny if they have good imaginations!

Does Christmas start too early?
Christmas shopping starts in September for some. UK High Streets start earlier each year and with more lavish commercialism than other nations. Is it just too commercialized? Is it appropriate? How does Christmas in your host country compare? Has it changed a lot in the past 20 years?

*Christmas TV/video recorder*

Students in groups have the TV pages for the UK for Christmas Eve-Boxing Day but just 1 TV in the house. Can they agree on which programmes/films to watch? Give them a grid with a choice of two possible programmes for each day (no more!)

Adapt this for lower levels. Give them a list of 10 programmes in simple language and they can record only four. Don't give them the page from the newspaper or TV magazine as it will overwhelm them. Set rules if you want: they must agree to record one film and one music programme. Alternative: make a list of the films which will be showing over the Xmas period. Ask each group to choose the best 3 films to watch.

Note: prepare all the vocabulary well for all types of students. What types of programmes do they like? Film drama soap operas What types of films do they know? Comedy thriller animated film Get examples of each programme type from the students.

*Choose the most appropriate card/gift*

Groups have a selection of cards/pictures of gifts and a list of people to give them to e.g. their teacher, boyfriend, grandmother... Can they agree on which is most suitable? Lots of cultural attitudes come out in this discussion. This is too challenging for lower levels. An alternative is to choose a present for yourself and say why you like it and then choose a present for someone else in the group and say why you think it is a good choice. This can be shorter and more controlled so could be used with lower levels. Always set up the activity by giving examples for yourself and inviting examples from the class.

*Internet links*

Search the news round site for Christmas resources and there is amazing scope for kids, lower secondary and lower levels. Very accessible stuff on diverse topics from the battle for the number 1 slot in the UK's Christmas charts and the Top 10 toys this year. What do news round users think? Does Xmas start too early? Great stuff here and not always too Christmassy for teens.

Look in holidays section for Christmas around the world. There's a good text on Christmas in England and Boxing Day customs/origins. The puzzles, word searches and crosswords are also suitable for lower levels with plenty of visual support. Use these puzzles as lesson starters or fillers. There is a good extract from 'A Christmas Carol' for higher levels and lots of simple stories to tell for lower levels and kids. The classroom games have some very useful ideas for language classes and the printable pictures are good too.

www.enchantedlearning.com/crafts/christmas/

A lesson on the history of Christmas trees which you could adapt and simplify or make a quiz on trees.

Photo credit: Caitlin, Volunteer in South Africa with African Impact Alum

This is a brilliant EFL game to practice giving

advice. It should be played after the 'giving advice' vocabulary lesson has taken place. It is a great way for students to see what they have remembered and what needs reviewing. This game works well with any age group, just adapt it to fit the age you're working with.

Why use it? Speaking and Listening; Giving Advice

Who it's best for: All ages and levels

How to play:

Write ailments or problems related to your most recent lesson on post-it notes and stick one post-it note on each student's back.

The students must mingle and ask for advice from other students to solve their problem.

Students should be able to guess their problem based on the advice they get from their peers.

Use more complicated or obscure problems to make the game more interesting for older students. For lower levels and younger students, announce a category or reference a recent lesson, like "Health", to help them along.

These games will keep your students engaged and happy as they learn! Remember, these are just ten on the hundreds of different EFL games that you can plate with your students. As you get more confident in the classroom, you can start putting your own spin on games and eventually make up your own.

Whatever the age of your students, they're guaranteed to love playing EFL games in the classroom. An EFL classroom should be fun, active and challenging and these games are sure to get you heading in the right direction.

This article was originally published in October 2013; we redesigned and updated this article in May 2018.

The following activities are designed to get everyone talking. They can be used with all levels because the language required to communicate is determined by the students.

Author: Clare Lavery

Remember to set up and demonstrate these activities carefully before letting the class go ahead.

*Jigsaw puzzle challenge*

Take 3-4 large pictures/photos and stick them on card. Pictures can come from Sunday supplements, travel brochures, calendars, magazine adverts etc. Pictures specific to students' interests will motivate them e.g. film stills, cartoons, news stories, famous paintings, famous people.

Nevertheless, teaching to adults can have also some less convenient aspects. The description of grownups is not so wonderful as it may be presented. Their world is full of duties, which they cannot resign from, like job or family. The lack of time can cause disadvantages noticeable during the lessons.

Above-mentioned expectations can turn into the criticism of teaching methods. According to Harmer (2007), their previous learning experience "may have predisposed them to one particular methodological style which makes them uncomfortable with unfamiliar teaching patterns." Furthermore, these learners can even become antagonistic towards some teaching and learning activities, similar to their earlier ones;

- being afraid of a failure is, according to Harmer (1998), another problem which adult learners has to deal with. They are anxious because criticism at school influenced on their self-confidence. Luckily, not all of them underachieved at school, those who succeeded may think that learning will be easy. Teachers can help to decrease the bad effects of past learning and the fear of failure by giving them attainable tasks;

- public embarrassment is another characteristic which is noticeable among adult learners. Their level of nervousness is high because they do not want to look ridiculously in front of the whole class. As pointed out by Harmer (1998), all these are related to the age "The potential for losing face becomes greater the older you get."

Offending behavior during the lesson is another problematic issue. They do not disturb in the same way as teenagers or children, but some grownups can spend a lesson on talking to each other at the same time when the teacher is trying to draw their attention. Some learners do not care about their homework or come late.

Boredom in class can occur even during the adults' lesson. It happens mostly because they, perhaps, are doing a full-time course or spending a lot of time in the same kind of classroom. According to Harmer, some kind of games or quizzes can be offered to these people. (Harmer, 1998)

To sum up, language learners differ to each other

not only in terms of age but also in terms of skills. They abilities, needs and even expectations change but characteristics, certainly specific to their age, play a crucial part in teaching.

In conclusion, some teaching methods are appropriate for particular age groups. Learners differ from each other and have special needs. The needs should always be provided sensibly in order to encourage students and do not repulse them. Choosing the suitable method teachers make that the students enjoy learning and do not associate it with something boring.

## CONCLUSIONS

The choice of the most appropriate teaching method, games and game-like activities has a significant importance to learners in different age groups; it is crucial to the learning process. Among many different methods and ideas for teaching, some of them are perceived as truly successful and efficient. The teacher's role is to find and tailor the best one and conform it to the particular learners' age.

The most effective ideas for teaching young learners are based on the TPR method. Its techniques and use of games and game-like activities constitute perfect conditions to acquire the language. Thanks to the briskness, appearing in most examples of games and game-like activities used in TPR method, children have the possibility to play, have fun and learn. What is more, pupils learn not because they have to but because they want to.

Teaching teenagers seems to be more challenging but equally rewarding. During the period of transition between childhood and adulthood, adolescents look for their identity and want to be as independent as possible. Thanks to some games and game-like activities, they are able to develop their creativity and increase their self-esteem. IT is rather difficult to motivate them, therefore, games have to be absorbing and related to the students' interests.

1. Adapted from New English File upper-intermediate Teacher's book by Oxenden et al. 2008: 221,225; (See Appendix 4)

2. Adapted from New English File upper-intermediate Teacher's book by Oxenden et al. 2008: 195,213; (See Appendix 5)

Adults represent the group of students who exactly know what they want to achieve. Although most of them are rather highly motivated the need to diversify lessons is still necessary. Quizzes based on general knowledge cause the improvement of students' language skills. Their life experience helps with the task, in which they have to describe specific situations or people.

In conclusion, appropriate teaching methods, techniques but also, really useful and effective, games and game-like activities are indispensible element of lessons. All of these components conduce to successful process of learning. That is why it is important to select them thoroughly and reasonably in terms of learners' abilities adapted to the particular age group.

# REFERENCES

1. Brown H. Douglas, 2007. Principles of language learning and teaching. Pearson Education. Fifth edition.
2. Halliwell Susan, 1992. Teaching English in the Primary Classroom. Longman Group UK Limited
3. Harmer Jeremy, 1998. How to teach English. Addison Wesley Longman Limited
4. Harmer Jeremy, 2007. The Practice of English Language Teaching. Pearson Education
5. Komorowska Hanna, 2005. Metodika nauzania jqzykow obcych. Warszawa: Fraszka Edukacyjna
6. Larsen-Freeman Diane, 2000. Techniques and principles in language teaching. Oxford University Press. Second Edition.
7. MacNaughton Glenda, Williams Gillian, 2004. Teaching young children. Choices in theory and practice. Open University Press.
8. One Stop English. Macmillan Publishers Ltd.
9. http://www.onestopenglish.com/teenagers/skills/games/teenagers-game-1-noughts-and-crosses/146729.article 2012-09-12 (last access)

10. One Stop English. Macmillan Publishers Ltd.

11. http://www.onestopenglish.com/teenagers/skills/games/teenagers-game-8-making-sentences/146736.article 2012-09-27 (last access)

12. Oxenden Clive, et al. 2008. New English File upper-intermediate Teacher's Book.

13. Oxford University Press

14. Osborne Priscilla, 2005. Teaching English One to One. How to teach one to one classes

15. for the professional English language teachers. Modern English Publishing.

16. Phillips Sarah, 1993. Young learners. Oxford University Press

17. Richards Jack C., Rogers Theodore S. 1986. Approaches and Methods in Language Teaching. Cambridge University Press

18. Toth Maria, 1995. Heinemann Children's games. Heinemann Publishers (Oxford)

19. Scott A. Wendy, Ytreberg H. Lisbeth, 1995. Teaching English to Children. Longman

20. Widodo Handoyo Puji, 2005. Teaching Children Using a Total Physical Response (TPR) Method: Rethinkign, Bahasa Dan Seni

21. Watcyn-Jones Peter, 1993. Vocabulary Games and Activities. Penguin Books Ltd

22. Wright Andrew, Betteridge David, Buckby Michael, 2006. Games for Language Learning. Cambridge University Press.

**Internet links**

1. http://benjaminzephaniah.com/ Information about the poet Benjamin Zephaniah. I haven't yet managed to work him into a lesson, but I think there's lots of potential to use his work in the classroom. Great for teenagers.

2. https://learnenglish.britishcouncil.org/en/stories-poems - The British Council's Learn English website has a huge archive of poems. You'll find any topic under the sun.

3. http://www.poemhunter.com/ this is a great site to help you find poems. It's especially useful if you can only remember a few lines.

4. http://www.bbc.co.uk/schools/gcsebitesize/english_literature/poetryrelationships/ - BBC bitesize website has some great resources for older teens

# APPENDICES

Appendix no. 1

Hello, Goodbye - the Beatles

You say yes, I say no,

You say stop, and I say go, go, go,

Oh no.

You say goodbye and I say hello, hello, hello,

I don't know why you say goodbye, I say hello, hello, hello,

I don't know why you say goodbye, I say hello.

I say high, you say low,

You say why, and I say I don't know.

Oh no.

You say goodbye and I say hello, hello, hello.

I don't know why you say goodbye, I say hello, hello, hello,

I don't know why you say goodbye, I say hello.

Why, why, why, why, why, why,

Do you say goodbye.

Oh no.

You say goodbye and I say hello, hello, hello.

I don't know why you say goodbye, I say hello, hello, hello,

I don't know why you say goodbye, I say hello.

You say yes, I say no,

You say stop and I say go, go, go.

Oh, oh no.

You say goodbye and I say hello, hello, hello.

I don't know why you say goodbye, I say hello, hello, hello,

I don't know why you say goodbye, I say hello, hello, hello,

don't know why you say goodbye, I say hello, hello, hello,


Appendix no. 2
  The example of a ready sheet of paper

Appendix no. 3

The example of the game: explaining what you mean (Harmer, 2007)

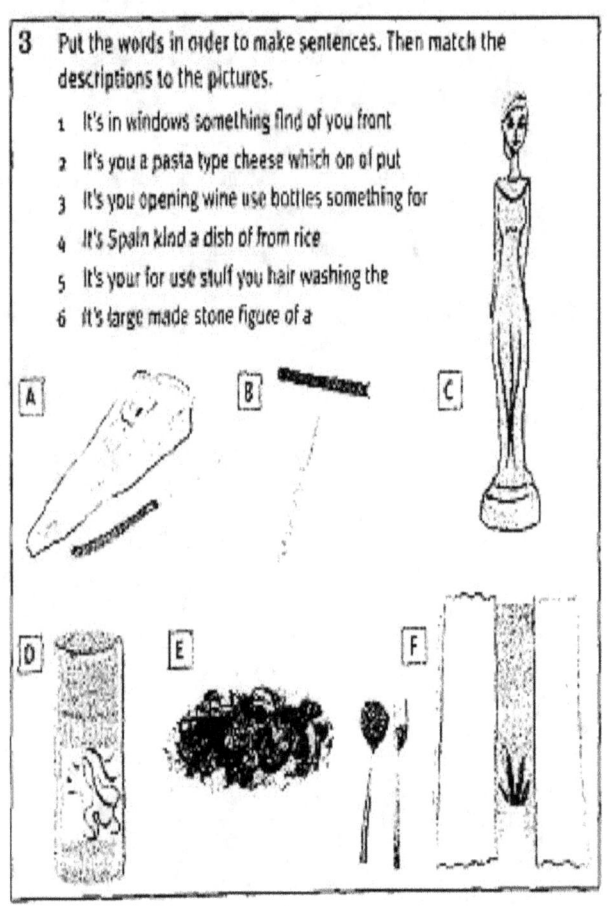

FIGURE 5: Practising 'explaining' words and phrases

Appendix no. 4

A describing game sheet (New English File upper-intermediate Teacher's book by Oxenden et al. 2008)

Appendix no. 5

A test sheet (Oxenden et al. 2008).

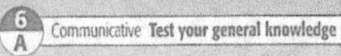

**6A** Communicative **Test your general knowledge**

**a** Complete the quiz with *a, an, the,* or – (no article).

**b** In pairs, see how many questions you can answer.

1 Which planet is nearest to ___ sun?
2 What type of fruit is ___ cantaloupe?
3 How many states are there in ___ USA?
4 In which sea can you find ___ Balearic Islands?
5 Who are more numerous in the world, ___ men or ___ women?
6 Which animal is ___ symbol of ___ WWF?
7 What colour are ___ babies' eyes at birth?
8 What is ___ 40% of 40?
9 What letter is on ___ right of ___ 'B' on a keyboard?
10 What was ___ name of ___ Tarzan's monkey?
11 What country is ___ Lake Como in?
12 What's ___ highest mountain in ___ Himalayas?
13 How many strings does ___ bass guitar have?
14 Who was ___ second person to walk on ___ moon?
15 How many players can be on court in ___ volleyball team?
16 What is ___ fourth sign of ___ zodiac?
17 Which nation first gave ___ women ___ right to vote?
18 Which animals were domesticated first, ___ cats or ___ dogs?
19 Which European country hasn't fought in ___ war since ___ 1815?
20 What is ___ largest man-made structure on Earth?
21 What vegetable is ___ vodka often made from?
22 Is ___ spider ___ insect?
23 What colour is ___ black box on ___ plane?
24 What's ___ sacred river in ___ India called?
25 Which travels faster, ___ light or ___ sound?

213

Appendix no. 6

A quiz (Watcyn - Jones, 1993).

''85 IT S QUIZ TIME: IDIOMS "

Read through the following questions and write your

88

answers on a separate piece of paper,

What kind of party is a stag party?

If you were at a restaurant and the person with you offered to go Dutch, what would this mean?

Our postman kicked the bucket last week. What has happened to him?

A tiresome, irritating person is often described as a pain in what part of the body?

Jim's behind bars. Where is he?

Amanda's down in the mouth today. How is she feeling?

Why wouldn't you normally go to a party in your birthday suit?

What sort of a relationship would you have with someone if you got on like a house on fire?

Why are blacklegs generally unpopular?

My uncle has been given a golden handshake. What has happened to him?

Where on the body would you find crow's feet?

How would you be behaving towards someone if you were giving him or her the cold shoulder?

What does a gate-crasher usually do?

How would you be feeling if you were full of beans?

Where (or what) would you be if you were in the land of Nod?

What's a busman's holiday?

What are you doing when you name the day?

What sort of person is an early bird?

Why don't people usually like playing gooseberry?

I've just bought the local rag. What have I bought?

www.ingramcontent.com/pod-product-compliance
Lightning Source LLC
LaVergne TN
LVHW010558070526
838199LV00063BA/5005